A Special Gift

Presented to:

From:

Date:

BLESSINGS OF ENCOURAGEMENT FROM PSALM 139

A Title in the Illuminated Treasures Series

Published by Multnomah Gifts™, a division of Multnomah Publishers, Inc.

© 2002 by The Forest Hills Group

International Standard Book Number 1-59052-016-5

Written by Matthew A. Price

Designed by Anderson Thomas Design

Scripture quotations are from:
The Holy Bible, New International Version ©1973, 1978, 1984
by International Bible Society, used
by permission of Zondervan Publishing House. All rights reserved.

Multnomah is a trademark of Multnomah Publishers, Inc., and is
registered in the U.S. Patent and Trademark Office.
The colophon is a trademark of Multnomah Publishers, Inc.

Printed in China

For information:
Multnomah Publishers, Inc.
Post Office Box 1720
Sisters, Oregon 97759

BLESSINGS OF
ENCOURAGEMENT
FROM
Psalm 139

Illuminated
Treasures
DISCOVERING THE LIGHT
OF GOD'S WORD

Multnomah Gifts™
Multnomah Publishers · Sisters, Oregon

Today, thankfully, the Bible is readily and affordably available to all who seek a daily relationship with Christ. Yet handy accessibility can also produce inattention to and underappreciation of the majesty and perfection of God's holy Word. Thus *Illuminated Treasures* is not simply a modern salute to the timeless tradition of artistically rendering Scripture. Its purpose ~ with images, design, and devotional text ~ is to draw you into the message of each verse and to bring you into a fuller awareness of how the Bible can apply to each situation, every circumstance, and all aspects of your life. May God richly bless you as you meditate on His Word and reflect on His perfect will for your life.

MATTHEW A. PRICE, *Winter 2001*

A History of Illuminated Texts

Imagine for a moment that the singular task you have chosen for the rest of your life is to hand copy the Bible, hymnals, or prayer books. Now imagine that your tools consist only of the trimmed flight feathers of a goose, a penknife, sable hairs, sand, and small sticks. Your inks are a combination of ground lapis lazuli, molten sulfur, corrosion from copper plates, and carbon black. Your parchment has taken weeks to produce as farmers have dried the hides of dozens of newborn calves through a careful, multistep process. ⊗ *F*inally you can begin inscribing the text ~ only you will not use the relatively easy method of carefully writing each word in clear, legible text. Instead you will painstakingly render each letter in calligraphic script, etch intricate designs around the borders, and draw elaborate pictures representing scenes and themes from the passages on the page. ⊗ *I*f this process seems unimaginable, then you can appreciate the world we live in, where books, magazines, and other reading materials are as common and plentiful as grass in a meadow. You can also see why before the advent of movable type, only institutions like the church and the very wealthy could afford to own a single book ~ or an illuminated manuscript as they are appropriately known. ❋ So you may be wondering, who would dedicate painful, solitary hours each day, each week, each month, for years on end to the task of producing a work that would only be appreciated by a select few? And what would inspire them to make this personal sacrifice? ❋

While some illuminated manuscripts were the products of paid artisans and craftsmen, the majority of the books produced prior to the thirteenth century were the handiwork of anonymous monks, canons, and nuns. For these dedicated scribes, remuneration and satisfaction came not from material gain or personal glory. Rather they labored in joyful service to their Lord. They held firm to the conviction that the Word of God, and the prayers and hymns written to praise Him, should be treated in such a manner that would highlight and celebrate the infinite importance of the text and effectively direct the reader's attention to the substance of key words and passages. ▨

Jesus, lover of my soul,

Let me to Thy bosom fly,

While the nearer waters roll,

While the tempest still is high:

Hide me, O my Saviour, hide,

Till the storm of life is past;

Safe into the haven guide;

O receive my soul at last.

CHARLES WESLEY
"Jesus, Lover of My Soul"

O LORD,
you have searched me
and you know me.

PSALM 139 : 1

You know when I sit and when I rise; you perceive my thoughts from afar.

PSALM 139:2

Every decision you make in life has consequences. Whether it's accepting a new job, attending a different church, or even something as mundane as paying the bills, your choices will affect your life and the lives of those around you. But always remember that Christians don't have to make decisions in a vacuum and then worry about what will happen next. If we earnestly seek God's guidance and diligently study His Word, God will direct our steps and keep us safe within His sheltering embrace.

Each minute of
the day has an eternity
that lies ahead and
an eternity that
has come before.
Yet never feel that
each moment in your
life is a small thing
in God's eyes. It is
upon these moments
that a lifetime is built,
and it was for each life
that turns to Him
that Christ paid
the price of salvation.

You discern my going out and my lying down; you are familiar with all my ways.

PSALM 139:3

Before

a word

is on my

tongue

you know it

you know it

completely,

O LORD.

PSALM 139:4

Words are amazing things. They can literally take on a life of their own, casting a shadow that endures for days, years, or even generations. Yet they have no physical substance whatsoever ~ no depth or breadth or height that can be measured. Truly there is nothing we as humans can create that has the power or the mystery of language. The Bible continually reminds us that with our words we can be a vehicle for enmity or peace, for dishonesty or integrity, for despair or hope. Pray that the words of your mouth are pleasing before the Lord and a source of encouragement to all who come face~to~face with these invisible but lasting expressions of your heart.

completely

You hem me in ~ behind and before; you have laid your hand upon me.

PSALM 139:5

In Philippians 4:6~7, Paul tells us, "Do not be anxious about anything, but in everything, by prayer and petition, with thanksgiving, present your requests to God. And the peace of God, which transcends all understanding, will guard your hearts and your minds in Christ Jesus." Despite hunger, imprisonment, and isolation Paul was able to encourage others because he never wavered in his conviction that God will ultimately provide for those who turn to Him.

Such knowledge is too wonderful for me, too lofty for me to attain.

PSALM 139:6

He leads us on by paths we do not know;

Upward He leads us, though our steps be slow,

Though oft we faint and falter on the way,

Though storms and darkness oft obscure the day;

Yet when the clouds are gone,

We know He leads us on.

NICOLAUS VON ZINZENDORF

Where can I go from your Spirit? Where can I flee from your presence?

PSALM 139:7

You are never alone. God is always standing between you and every challenge, every sorrow, every fear. As David said in Psalm 28:7, "The LORD is my strength and my shield; my heart trusts in him, and I am helped."

If I go up to the heavens, you are there; if I make my bed in the depths, you are there.

PSALM 139:8

I looked at God and He looked at me, and we were one forever.
CHARLES HADDON SPURGEON

A common reaction to the disappointments, the sorrows, and the unfortunate vagaries of life is to believe that God has callously forsaken us to an unhappy and unjust fate. For some this feeling of abandonment can produce anger and resentment; for others a search for personal fault produces guilt and depression. While it's impossible from our human perspective to understand the reasons behind or the resolution for every experience, event, or circumstance, we can rest assured that God can redeem anyone, anywhere, in any situation. The loving embrace of Christ's atonement is as vibrant and available to all who call on His name today as it was two thousand years ago when He invited a dying man who had reached the lowest depths of human experience to join Him that day in paradise.

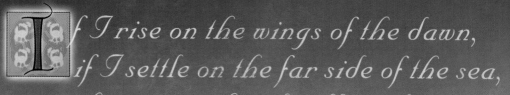

If I rise on the wings of the dawn,
if I settle on the far side of the sea,
even there your hand will guide me,
your right hand will hold me fast.

PSALM 139:9~10

If I say, "Surely the darkness will hide me and the light become night around me," even the darkness will

the darkness will

not be dark to you; the night will shine like the day, for darkness is as light to you.

PSALM 139:11~12

not be dark to you

Sun of my soul,

Thou Savior dear,

It is not night if Thou be near;

O may no earthborn cloud arise

To hide Thee from Thy servant's eyes!

JOHN KEBLE
"Sun of My Soul"

$\int$t is a marvelous

thing to know

that before the

foundations of

the earth were laid,

God knew us

and loved us.

For you created
my inmost being;
you knit me together
in my mother's womb.

PSALM 139:13

I praise you because
I am fearfully and
wonderfully made;
your works are
wonderful, I know
that full well.

PSALM 139:14

Before we were able to walk, to speak, to have opinions,
to have likes and dislikes, God knew us and loved us. . . .

Before we accepted His Son as our Lord and Savior, God knew us and loved us....

made in

My frame was not hidden from you
the secret place
when I was made in the secret place.

PSALM 139:15

When I was woven together in the depths of the earth, your eyes saw my unformed body.

PSALM 139:15

*A*nd now, this very day,
we are like a flower blossoming
under the warmth of His loving gaze . . . .

And for all the days to come,
for all of eternity, we have the
assurance ~ the blessed assurance ~
that God, our Heavenly Father,
will care for us, protect us, and bind
us to Him as His everlasting bride.

All the days
ordained for me
were written
in your book
before one of them
came to be.

PSALM 139:16

How precious to
me are your
thoughts, O God!

How vast is

How vast is the
sum of them!

PSALM 139:17

O Lord, our Heavenly Father, You are the author of all good and perfect things. In You and You alone may we abide in serenity and comfort and joy. Although no one can with certainty know what the future will hold, all can rest in and be assured by the knowledge that You are in control and that all things will be accomplished within the bounds of Your perfect will. Increase our faith, O Lord, and grant us the peace that passeth all understanding. In the precious name of Your Son, our Saviour, Jesus Christ, we pray, amen.

the sum of them!

I have believed in the Son of God, for He alone is the end of salvation, and the basis of immortal life; for He is a refuge to the tempest~tossed, a solace to the afflicted, a shelter to the despairing.

THECLA, A CHRISTIAN IN THE EARLY CHURCH

Were I to count them,
they would outnumber
the grains of sand.
When I awake,
I am still with you.

PSALM 139:18

If only you would slay the wicked, O God!

Away from me, you bloodthirsty men!

They speak of you with evil intent;

your adversaries misuse your name.

Do I not hate those who hate you, O LORD,

and abhor those who rise up against you?

I have nothing but hatred for them;

I count them my enemies.

PSALM 139:19~22

In recent years many well~known social commentators, pundits, and critics have made it fashionable to decry any expression of moral outrage as an unsophisticated reaction that is ill~mannered, uncivil, and (worst by far) unfairly judgmental. To believe in absolutes that have been laid out by an all~knowing and all~powerful God is, for many, not only naïve but also tantamount to declaring war on the foundation of our democracy. All of this is simply the latest spin on Satan's oldest lie. Christ commanded us to love our enemies, but the Bible also stresses that believers are to turn from and hate that which is unholy and impure. Don't let the snares of secular wisdom lull you into complacency and tolerance for anything that is an affront to God. Be steadfast in your convictions and place your love for Christ and His Kingdom above your desire to be in vogue.

Perfect submission, all is at rest,

I in my Savior am happy and blest;

Watching and waiting, looking above,

Filled with His goodness, lost in His love.

FANNY J. CROSBY
"Blessed Assurance"

Search me, O God,
and know my heart;
test me and know my
anxious thoughts.

PSALM 139:23

Our image as Christians is not merely what we can see in our reflection in a mirror, but is cast in the expanding glory of Christ's presence in our lives and the encouragement we feel when we become more and more like Him each day.

See if there is any offensive way in me, and lead me in the way everlasting.

PSALM 139:24

Expect great things from God;
attempt great things for God.

WILLIAM CAREY

God's refining touch is not always
quick and very seldom easy, yet if
we utterly submit to His guiding
hand we will experience a sense
of fulfillment that can never be
gained through personal attempts
at self~improvement or public
glory. Open your heart to Christ's
life~changing presence. Only
He can bring you true peace
and lasting encouragement.

May our Lord Jesus Christ himself
and God our Father,
who loved us and by his grace gave us
eternal encouragement and good hope,
encourage your hearts and strengthen
you in every good word and deed.

2 THESSALONIANS 2:16~17